Int

The purpose of this hand book is to answer a question that is more and more asked by video gamers. How do I start packaging an idea for a video game in a demo and put it out there? In Fact 165.000.000 of Americans play video games, and the average age seems to be about 30+. So in fact a lot a gamers have this nudge for getting creative and make a video game themselves, even just for fun. The problem to this matter is that in every other industry there is a method to put your ideas out there and get attention. The most classic is a business plan that you expose to the bank for a loan. Or in Hollywood, the standard of treatments, to sell your concept for a none-written script. But it the video game industry there is no standard, there is no method for producing a demo.

I believe that if there is no standard for demonstrations it is because nobody has aced it yet. But I have faith that with 165 million players, all in their adulthood; some guys are going to get smart and make the standard. Besides, making a demo for a presentation could easily become a finished game that could be sold as an app. And one could start from that entry in to the craft then grow exponentially. Everything is possible; this is a huge, very dynamic industry. All you need is to be able to organize your ideas; the passion will do the rest.

As a hard core gamer who has been there from the beginning of this industry, the mid 70's. And really enjoyed it passionately; I will expose all that is necessary to be able to visualize the concept and make it happen as a valid game. Meaning we will explore all the technicalities and details, that in fact make any video game appealing

In this effort we will cover all the different type of games with their particular game-play. And also all the creative details that have become a "must have" in each of this standards. We will also cover as much detail as possible in the art directing as it is the key to success for video games. May be one of the most important points. So we will in fact be studying the production values of video games. Meaning the inputs to be done in detail to have a video game become a hit.

We will also discuss all the different approaches to art directing that one could use to make the game more approachable from a production or a marketing point of view. Meaning different approaches to create the game that make better sense for the platform and the game type.

With this approach , we will always start with the concepts of the game type from the broader point of view. First as a game for consoles, with all the power and memory needed. Then we will explore the same approach, from the perspective of smaller platforms such as smart phones and tablets. As these are becoming a new standards. Plus, they are the most approachable for the first production.

Also I will not use examples of video games . Because if I start using a game from the early 80's as an example; probably nobody is going to get it. I will visually and plainly describe everything that needs to be done. So that new gamers can get properly inspired.

At each specific point of the reading, I will give a full list of all the things that the producer needs to get done. And a method on how to concretize the most elaborate parts. Thus, from this reading's perspective , the creator must have already a full story in mind. From the beginning to the end, and with a full plot. Yet we will cover all the points needed to adapt a story to a tail for video games.

Then after all this material has been covered, and the reader has a good perspective on exactly what he needs to pursue from a production point of view and gets started with the project. We will cover the best avenues to make it happen and put it out there. I will discuss all the different possibilities to gather the resources that you need. And, optimize the production value in all aspects to build the game. Even explore different methodologies to find sponsoring for the game, by including it in the concept from the start.

Chapter 1 : Conceptualization:

Different type of games.

Game-play.

Story-lines.

Locations and environments.

Time-lines & planning process.

Imagination at work.

Chapter 2 : Art Directing & Creative Process:

Character creation.

Color Palette and Ambiance.

Backgrounds.

Game-play & Immediate Environment

Inventory and items

Sounds & Music

Animation

Polishing the content of the game.

Synchronization : The Secret Kung Fu

Chapter 3: Optimizing production for market reach and maximum appeal:

Production : Simplify.

Optimizing production.

Getting funds to complete the project.

Chapter 1:

Conceptualization

To do list:

Read and assimilate all the material.

Choose a game type for your project.

Pick a good story for your game.

Brainstorm and note down your ideas.

Make the story fitting to your game type.

Note ideas about game-play and animations.

Note ideas about story-lines and story adaptations.

Take notes to insert awesome environments.

Take notes to insert awesome locations.

Take notes about your characters as they come.

Start creating your story-line and your time-line for the whole game.

Use the social medias (or else) to find a good hand drawer (Sketcher). With art designing attributes.

Start making lists of all the tasks that need to be done for production step by step.

Get a blog going on your project.

Start looking into the investment site operating on the net for financing small projects. Understand how they function.

Get started with the first drawings.

Different type of games :

Sports Games

The most popular genre of game are sports games. That is all of them. But they all must have some same standards, which we explore in the section about game-play. Sports games are usually directed straight towards the love of the game, as a pure enjoyment for the action in the sport. Therefore game-play is everything if you are pursuing this concept. In general the art directing goes all towards the realism of the official league teams.

Making a sports game for hand devices, could in fact be very successful if it is done properly. Many different approaches can be considered. Like using puppies or babies for characters in a game of tennis on a hand device. If the art directing, the synchronization and the game-play are good. One might be surprised to see the success of his little game.

Role Playing Games /RPG

The second most popular genre of games are the role playing games. They come usually in three different types. The most classics are in an open environment where the avatar can evolve freely and unfold the script of the game. The same concept is doing a rage in online communities where teams come together to play levels. Then they hang around in the virtual towns, playing cards and exchanging items.

In these games, the player can accomplish a multitude of tasks. He can do commerce by collecting items or investing in businesses, buy real estate , build relationships and more. Plus have different ways of locomotion, even taking a cab, driven by an actual player on-line. These games also have a multitude of environments and places to explore. Usually they are action and adventure directed for the game-play. But the complexity of the universe in which the player evolves and customizes the avatar to himself , is the most appealing part of the game. This genre of game is often a block buster.

The second most popular of role playing games are shooter games. Where the avatar experiences the universe from a first person point of view. The story-lines are much shorter with the pace of a movie script. And the game-play is much more dynamic. More action directed. This type of game must have a good story to carry it, or it is not going to make it.

For RPG shooter ; the action is in fact half of the game. Don't get me wrong , the action game-play must be perfect. With all the cool arsenal and inventory that make these games a standard. Nice guns controls and artificial intelligence for the enemies is crucial. Today most of the interesting shooters have the avatar carry a weapon in his right hand. And use magic from the left hand, like holding a voodoo artifact to jinx and put spells on the enemies. This is becoming more and more common with shooters , it adds a lot to the aspect of the game-play because it allow to have some nice alternatives using the spells and it gives personality to the game. The spells at the disposal are always a full part of the side story, and help for the synchronicity of the game-play with the main story. So it must be available in the game if it makes sense with the plot line.

Yet, the whole universe behind the action is the main achievement of the game. In an RPG shooter the story and the characters aptitudes are more in emphasis. Each level must tell a chapter of the story with fine animations and good story telling. And the accomplishments in the levels must give attribute points for the characters aptitudes to make the avatar faster and better. Secret levels and secret locations with goodies are always a plus for this type of games. It is strongly recommended to put plenty in the levels with relevant items in them. To taunt the player to play the level till he gets all the bonuses.

The ability to jump, run, and position, the character with precision is a full part of the game-play. This approach to gaming is very good for spy or horror games with an elaborate plot like in a novel. It must have a good artificial intelligence for the enemies. Very often shooters are criticized because of the lack of efficiency in the AI .

The enemies, even if monsters, must have an intelligent and realistic behavior during the fights, and have their own different body languages in the animation. If the story is good, the engine is fluid, the game will find an audience and have sequels .

The third kind of role playing games are the most ancient ones. Where the gamer is presented with just one picture on the screen. And every time the character turns around he sees the picture on his left or his right and so forth. With the mouse, (sometimes with the out most precision), he must find the clues in these pictures to go through the levels and unfold the story.

Most of these games are based on investigative scripts. Like murders and mysteries. The game does not have to be very slow, that depends on the story-line. The sounds in this type of games is a full part of the ambiance. The more details in the sounds, the more the activities in the picture become alive. It is like a reminiscence of books for children. May be that is why the most famous ones of these games where very scary, and became collectible standards.

Also in this genre , there is some nice little games that are based on a cartoon animation, they do very well for kids and chicks alike. Basically the player can see the character on the screen like in a cartoon and can either go left or right to un-scroll the environment . And use the mouse pointer to move the guy or investigate the locations. Those games when they come with a full story and nice artistic palette are pretty net. It would be perfect for a hand devices. With some nice graphics and nice magical tales, it is a perfect way to tell a story. And also a project that could be done by one guy only. It is the oldest, and the simplest way to make an RPG. It is still valid, if the puzzles and the clues in the game do not drive the player nuts. That's the trick , the player must be able to finish the game.

Puzzle Games

Puzzle games are candy, they have always been. That is the intent. Very popular, these games are all about synchronicity and artistic inputs. They are very easy for production. They include also all the games of cards and casino.

Using a good old game of backgammon but making it futuristic, like the pawns are nanobots one a mother board. Trying to infiltrate the main system. Is an example of the kinds of variations that will always be appealing to those who play these games. Because they get to experience it from a different ambiance. And ambiance is the key seller for a puzzle game. Keep this in mind.

 Some puzzle games now are considered as "brainers". Meaning they are suppose to make you smarter of sorts. This approach is in fact very popular. Pursuing this new use of puzzles in the gaming industry gets a lot of heat from within the industry itself. But the marketing is a bit of a hassle. Those games bring good Etiquette. Which might help for production and financing. But they must be scientifically backed up.

Strategy Games

Strategy games are very common; in fact they are all over the place. The ambiance is the main seller in this genre. All those strategy games happen in a different age, time, and space.   They are often directed towards commanding troops in battle and infrastructure evolution from exploiting resources. The other approach is based upon only evolution. Where the player is in fact growing a civilization. Or strange creatures living in a strange environment. One could get very imaginative with this approach on strategy games about what is being shepherd by the gamer, and make a new genre within the genre. It happens all the time.

Game-play is important for strategy games. The multiplicity of the actions that the player can take, makes the quality of the game. And that means a lot of parameters. The more, the better. Parameters inputs on construction, social events, economic happenings, weathering, war and so forth. Adding smart factors in the economic parameters and show the population change habits or items is in fact part of the game-play for this genre of games. Even those directed on battle must have the quality of their weaponry evolving. So all this little details, are more than just details for strategy games. They are part of the game-play synchronization.

Menu access is very important for these games. Everything is often done threw a menu. They all offer key board short cuts. But still, the menu is always in use. So the quality and the design of the menu interface is also a full part of the game-play for strategy games. The player must be able to perform his commands and surf menus in real time.

Some strategy games are action shooters, They are pretty cool. Basically the player is moving a team of 5 to eight characters on the field, just by clicking the mouse on where he wants the character to position himself; then chooses the action to take till orders change.

Like spy operatives on an infiltration operation. Or five mercs on a battle field. The point is to move the characters to strategic point in the map to progress in the level. These games are very nice because they allow none experienced players to get a good sense of thrill, and action with a soft game-play without going nuts on the controls. And they usually have very elaborate story, as if straight out of Hollywood.

Simulation Games

These are usually directing towards experiencing driving or flying from the most realistic, and professional point of view.

Sometimes, sports games are also presented as simulation. Like golf for instance. This category of games is the hardest type to produce. As a simulation game, the parameter adjustments and the engine to carry the game must be at their optimum. And the producer must get a license deal to be able to use brands that are actually real.

Some simulations get very creative by transposing actual simulation with funky concepts like miniature cars racing in a baby room or other creative approaches. With the addition of this type of arcade mode , this games do very well.

In General :

Most of all the famous role playing games mix all the different types of categories . For instance the use of simple puzzles in action games is very common. Like used as game-play for by-passing circuits to open doors, or hacking computers. Even to build new items on a tool bench. The use of this method is in fact a "must have" for role playing games. They give a brake and some time to relax before jumping back in the action. Also the use of driving and flying is now always there for RPGs, especially those of a contemporary age. They are even very simulation directed. The mixing of genre is in fact becoming the new genre of Role playing games. It is important to perceive this from a producer's angle and always look for a rational way to make that input.

Realism must always be there in every type of game. The details of the games universe must be as complete as the platform can allow it. The environment must be alive with synchronicities of nature and human interactions. The quality of the graphics for the game must be done with beauty and "bling" .The quality of commands for driving and flying must be perfect. And also the response of the environment to all that is happening must be realist. The chain effect of things must be fluid and pretty to the eye. Those are the points that are the real concern for the production on any game.

All the different type of games are also present for hand devices. The main difference would be that because of platform restrictions, the production value is more based on an "arcade" approach. So for hand devices all type of games must be more inclined toward a certain past of game-play for the enjoyment of the player .There is just not enough room on the screen or in the hard ware to accomplish any other kind of elaborate games. And in theory people would not spend hours playing on their phones. At least not in public.

Puzzle games with an arcade inclination are the most common for hand devices. Also good old platform games do pretty well when the game-play and the controls are smart.

So in fact a good platform game with a good story and interesting puzzles would be the best way to make an RPG/action for hand devices.

Most of the RPGs on hand devices are represented from an up view angle. There are some RPGs that are all in 2D animations looking like 3d, offering a world to explore to the player. And some others are entirely in 3D; from the big game makers. But there are more interesting ways to accomplish this. Methods that we will discuss later with other points.

So in fact hand devices even though limited; could be perfect for making adventure games by mixing genres. And of course any kind of arcade game based on an 80's approach, like a flipper, or a car game where you see the car un-scroll the scenery , are still loads of fun.

Just it is essential to understand that the production value of the game would be in its arcade aspect and graphic appeal .

<u>Game-play</u>

All different categories use a different type of game-play. That is the essence of video gaming. Players are attracted to different types of game-plays. For instance women are more inclined towards strategy and puzzles rather than high past shooters. Some people really enjoy the slow past of strategy game; other can't get enough of fast past action shooters full of gore.

So the quality of the game-play must be an accomplishment in itself. It is the first point to master in this craft. The aim of a game-play is to be pleasant. It is very simple, the player must feel fully in control of his character. Not the environment, at least not entirely. But when it comes to the avatar the fluidity of actions and the speed of movement are very important. If the player feels that he is trying to move in deep sand it will aggravate the gamer. Plus the accessibility to the menus and inventories must also be very fluid, and organized in the most optimized way. If the player can fly threw his menu and inventory, it will add to the sensation of control.

In essence the purpose of any game-play is to enable the gamer to act in the game as fast as he can think. That is the purpose of game-play, it must be there. The command responses must fallow this very important rule. For all genres, on all platforms. I cannot stress enough the importance of this in gaming.

Sports games , for instance, take the game-play to the edge. Not only the commands must be responsive but the game must be designed so that the player has always a proper field of vision of the play ground and the team around him. Putting the game-play in synchronization with the camera is part of the game-play. So camera positioning is the second most important point of game play. In a good game, there are usually different point of view proposed to the player. Like Close, near, or far. Some sports and strategy games, now offer a third person view for experiencing the game with some action shooter game-plays.

The command response parameters must also be redefined every time that the point of view changes. When it is a far point of view, some controls need to be loosened a little bit, and thither on closer angles. So this part of making a game is something that the creator must be aware of: The tricks of game-play time response. But game-play is also about organizing the play ground with funning games.

Some shooter games present two variation of the game-play. You can choose arcade mode or realistic. Arcade mode is usually a way to expand the game by proposing challenges. Like replaying the levels unlocked, and experience it again with a more garnished serving. Like the level is suddenly a ghost town and the character is reliving it in a night mare. Or it is a last man standing challenge with a time trial. And playing this arcade levels, will unlock memories or specials for the character. It is very cool to have a nice arcade mode with crazy creative inputs.

 Plus these arcade level must have some of that "bling" of the old days , like points popping out of the targets with a jackpot sound or any kind of aspect that made arcade games awesome in the 80's. In fact a good arcade mode is trying to make the junction between the modern aspects of precision gaming with all the funky aspect that was the essence of video games in the early age.

An "arcade" mode is about goodies to get more and more outrageous scores and achievements rewards. As opposite to the story mode (or realistic mode), where the game has to be directed towards realism, to maintain the thrill of the story-line. Sometimes the command controls in arcade mode are faster and easier. But not always. It is most often in sports games, and car games where the arcade more is proposed, with a more simplified control and easier game-play . It is to give levels with an immediate access to the action, not going through the process of choosing team, or picking cars. And the accomplishment of this arcade modes are also used to unlock goodies for the pro mode. Like customizations and money to buy equipment.

Slow motions are also used more often in the game-play. Athletes, and professional gunmen, do in fact sense a moment where they transcend time and space right before they throw the ball or pull the trigger. So it is used in the game-play by slowing down time, and zooming the focus just on the action to be performed. The slow motion time is limited and must be regained by scoring points in the game. This is becoming a real standard in all action games, even car games.

A slow motion mode to do the precision driving needed to get under a truck at 189 miles per hour. To just, push the other opponent from the right point to get his car flipping. Is a very nice touch for car games. This new controls add to the game-play possibilities and makes the game more interesting. Even on simulations.

In shooter games the slow motion allows the game to be filled with more targets and enemies. It is in fact a "must have" in shooters it really gives a nice aspect to the action thrill. With usually the sound of a pounding hart during the slow motion to simulated the adrenaline rush. This method is used also in hand to hand combats during final battles or a cinematic. Where you have a slow down to allow you to perform the actions. Actions that are supposed to be very fast like dodging a bullet or a commando knife fight. Slow motions are also used more and more on level bosses. They are used to enable the character to shoot at inaccessible points or even climb on the monsters to strike. Slow motions are pretty net. They are becoming standard.

There are new aspects to RPG's, which are to be considered as game-play. It is the gathering of Organic materials or scavenging parts. Like plants and other strange things. Then use a lab to mix the ingredients and make potions. Or a tool benches to optimize weapons and armors. This new type of game-play, brake the pace of the game, to allow for a pause. So that the character can regroup, and build up his character. So the quality of this labs or benches is becoming a full part of RPGs. The use of a simple puzzle can be implemented to accomplish the actions in these labs, or work benches. But they must be simple and easy.

There is also a new type of game-play that you see sometimes. It is a game-play that is not based on usually action, or adventure. The game-play is more directed towards social happenings and parameters. For instance the player has to nourish a whole family in a house. Take care of each individual by giving them social interactions to do, and make sure that their level of satisfaction is high. Like going to school, take showers, take care of the house. Dress up to go out on a date, and more. Basically like playing with a doll house.

To give you another example for this type with a plot. The character is living in a one world order environment. And he must talk to people to organize and start a revolution to save the country. So the game-play is all about scouting the city, to spot the right people to recruit. Organize secret meeting, covering the operations, and financing the movement. This unique games do in fact have a following. But to design one, is like designing a new board game. It is hard to come up with new game-plays that are unique and really fun. But if one would ace this; he would probably create a whole new genre in the gaming industry and establish a new standard. So if you're hungry for making it in this business, keep this in mind.

As we established, game-play is about command control. For consoles and pc games the controls are quit efficient. But on smaller platforms it is a tricky matter.

Usually for a smaller platforms, the interaction interface is ribboned on the side or under the screen. The problem then is to make sure that the fingers would fit. The best trick is to use a circle with one other circle inside it and other buttons on the sides as needed. The circular movements of the finger (or a screen pen) on the big circle in the middle will direct the movements of the character or the car. Tapping in the outer ring as you direct the avatar allows for shooting. Or controlling the speed of movement or any other type of quick action. And the thumbs on the other hand can handle the other action buttons.

Although this example inspires to be universal. For these smaller platforms, one might need to create something that is custom made for his game. For example, if it was a tennis game for a hand device. It would make better sense to put the interaction interface at the top the screen. So that the phone is properly balanced in the hand for a better control. And the left button on the left for the left thumb, and right button on the right for the right hand. A slide on the button could trigger the type of ball the player wants to make. Lobs, straight shots or else. So a first pressure on the button would make the character run, and then a slide of the thumb would assign the kind of ball hit desired. What I am trying to say here, is that getting creative with the control interface for hand devices is most applauded.

Optimizing this type of control panels is the very important for making a game on small platforms. It must be responsive and practical. A standard in the execution for this particular problematic in the industry; has yet to be defined.

The best way to make a command panel for a game on hand device is as fallow. Make a translucent ribbon on the top or bottom of about 18 % of the screen. On the far left put four buttons in a cross, exactly like the game pads of the early consoles. One for each direction. It is the best way so to keep the thumb in place and note all over the place. On the right side put the buttons for action. Make them small, like the ones for texting, but make them spaced from each other. In addition every time that the player pushes on the commands he must get a vibrational response from the device to simulate the clicking action. In doubt, keep this configuration for your game so the game-play is enjoyable. Most app have a disastrous command system, it is almost disgraceful to the consumer.

Story-lines

The story-line is like the script of the game. RPGs have a much more elaborate story with an entire plot . But some puzzles also have a story. For instance the pawn to move are rocks blocking the passage of ants . So when the puzzle is solved all the ants can go to the hive. This is a little scenario for the puzzles that immediately gives production value to the game. It opens extra game-play variations, using ants to personalize the levels.

Or imagine an American football game where the players are ,again, babies and puppies. With their helm and their diapers, standing in formation. And as they are "babies" they can't really run straight without tumbling. And the football is twice the size of their heads any way . So they can't really carry it far. It's a circus on the field .But they are really trying hard. This little story is a full script for a football game. In fact, very fit for a hand device build with a fast pace arcade game-play, full of goodies and pop-ups.

So there must always be a story for any game of any genre. Like flippers. Some people never understood that there is a story to the flipper. One should not just hit the ball randomly. Following the scores to take in the right sequences. Leads, to more and more challenging bonuses. Till you might find yourself screaming:

" Yeah ! I succeeded three of Zeus's challenges in only two hours. I am looking good! ".

That madness because the story-line of the flipper is taking the better of you. I cannot stress this enough; if there is no story, the game is going to be dull. Probably a failure.

Adventure role playing games must have a very long and elaborate story . Some RPGs, just start with the avatar standing in an great environment with a perfect game-play. But he must go around to start quests and missions. So the game does not give the impression to have a main story-line; just a bunch of side stories that might come together or not.

Well; this approach won't hit the market the same way, as if the game would start with an animation that presents the story of the game.

The quality of the beginning's animation and directing; is what will make the appeal to the game. It must have all the drama and the appropriate presentation for the characters in the context of the story. It must give a clear impression of the main character, and also the main bad guy plus one or two of his capos. The first animation must also expose the emotional object of the story. Damsels in distress or terrorists plots, make your pick. The garnishing of the directing and the look of the animation must look like a super production from Hollywood. It makes the overall production value of the RPG.

Exactly like in script writing for Hollywood. The plot must have a very appealing main story, or "A" story. And the "A" story must fit in a "B" story and may be a "C" plot, if there is room . In TV shows for example, the numbers of side stories keep going on and on.

This principle must be applied to the story writing for an RPG. It is within the standard. An RPG adventure game must have a minimum of "A" To "D" story layers in the plot . (Or story-lines). All the different plots will lead to different places for the player to see and play the game. So they carry the momentum of the game-play.

The "A" story will unfold at a slow past threw the various quest and missions. Those side quests are independent ,and may be different with unique characters and scripts. Like a little story of it own.. So these are the "B" stories, that the writer is using to unfold the "A" story.

The "C" story would be quests that are given by characters, that are not, part of the "A" story or "B" Story-lines. They are like thresh hold guardians. Their quests usually have a different purpose than the main story, like horror or magic stuff. So the "C" story-line comes together to be in fact the "B" story of the original script. The "C" line offers special items , and special attribute for the player. Like a self discovery journey.

But get more creative than that. Because the "B" story of the game (or the "C" story-line) is the aspect that gives the most blush to the production value of the game as far as, a good story telling goes. Exactly like in Hollywood.

Imagine a "A" story about mobsters happening in that specific universe. With all kinds of "B" stories related to that world. But the "C" story-line; is in fact unfolding a voodoo curse that is killing the guy so he must hurry. That is the most proficient way to use this method. Anything to enlarge the game, and bring in more imagination, plus adding alternative game-plays like Guns and cursing at the same time.

The "D" story-line is also a "must have" for elaborate RPGs. This "D" Line should be designed to make the universe of the game attaching to the player. Like a friendship with a guy running a shop throughout the game. That will, if well " played", get the character a special quest with some seriously awesome goodies. These "D" stories are used to make the player bound with the universe and the characters around him. It all about immersing the player in the ambiance of the game.

Some "D" stories are short. Just about assisting people and become more popular. Some are more intriguing and harder to sequence . Like a treasure hunt, but with only clues marked on trees and that's it ,no other clues . It could also be a love affair leading to a successful wedding, or a romantic disaster.

Writing this complex kind of scenario for a video-game is going to require some story engineering. That means , to interlink those different story-line within each other, so that they become a full story that makes sense. There are some rules to follow.

Any plot can be very easily adapted to a video-game. Every time that a character in plot is changing location. That is game-play. Every time that the first character in an plot is on momentum, that is game-play. So if the plot is happening in a train, then the game would be about getting to the "plot-point" where the story unfolds, by running into game-play adventures on the way to the wagon describe in the book. Understanding this very simple rule is all you need to adapt any novel into a video-game. The art directing is to come up with some creative adventures to make to playable parts. The action points or "B" Stories on the way to the wagon, would be quests with their own little story. In a novel those story won't be there. So the creation of these "B" to "D" stories must fit as much as possible with the contents of the original plot. Usually those quest are very game-play directed, but one talented writer could get very creative with this unique approach to storytelling.

For a very elaborate RPG, the Main story should be organized ,(as an example) , in 13 chapters. Each level of the game becomes a full chapter of the story. Each chapter should have at least 7 to 10 "B" side stories , to lead the telling of the main story and the finish of the chapter. And in addition there should be 5 to 7 "C" side stories. Plus an extra of at least 4+ "D" side stories. As these latter, give life longitude to the game.

The "A" story must be told with animations. It is quite important. Each chapter should have a few short , but very high quality, animations about the drama of plot "A". Till the finish of the chapter, that must end with a longer and more elaborate animation. These animations to tell the story, must have all the characters involved in the main plot. If any characters of the main plot is going to die in the script. It must happen during one of the animations with all the drama effect. The last piece of the animation that will conclude the game at the end. Is very crucial.

Like any good movie , the game must end properly. A long animation with high quality , that will conclude all the loose ends. And also present all the character of the main plot , coming to some sort of a happy ending. Or maybe not so happy. As most games will give a multiple endings to the main plot. All regarding the choices made in the game. So there is usually two to three different ending to the main plot in a good RPG. Its sounds like a lot of extra work. But not really , because the other side stories are constant.

The "B" story-line is usually build by blocks of independent stories. Quests that are given by the main characters in the game, in order to establish trust or so. As such; they will eventually undisclosed information that will unfold the "A" Story-line. This is a classic method . But to complete it; each of these "B" side stories must have some secret items or archives that are revealing more deeper information about what is really going on it the main story. That is how these "B" stories are always carrying; threw their execution, the telling of the main story. Of course it is better to have some of the "B" Stories be directly link to the main story, but not always.

The "B" story-lines are where the game is actually going to be played and experienced. So the missions and the quests must be long and smart, with a good design. The Artificial intelligence must be up to the task, and present different types of way to corner the character.

The "C" stories must be initiated by characters that the avatar is going to have to find; or often that are just going to walk up and give a secret message. "C" stories must give the impression to immerse the character in a second universe within the main one. So the presentation of these particular levels, must always stand alone in the game. For instance exploring a dungeon in ruins, or dealing with a haunted house; all this happening in an RPG ,initially about the Second World War. The immersion of the character from one universe to the other must be felt completely.

The "B" line and the "C" line should not coincide. They should be independent from each other's content. But it is recommended to use characters introduced in the "B" story-line to build "D" story-lines. Like personal relation's or may be even conflicts to shake things up.

The "C" line events, must stand alone and be brought in the main plot at the discretion of the production. As the completion of this "C" levels will grant new powers and aptitudes to the player. They need to be played at specific points in the game to allow the completion of some "B" levels.

All these different quest and missions must be designed, so that the player gets to explore as much as possible the universe that is proposed to him.

To give an example. Take the first chapter of the plot and divide it in 4 different points, so the story of the first chapter in the plot will be told in four successive parts. The "A" story in a video-game is always going to be communicated with the use of animations during the levels, or text when conversing with main characters.

So the first draw of the story-line is going to look very simple. Draw a line and mark on the line, A1 then leave some room and mark A2 and so on till A4. Call this first line "A" Story-line chapter 1.

Then draw under the first line a second parallel line call it "B" story-line , Between A1 and A2 , Place B1 and then B2. So the Character is going to have to play B1 and B2 before he gets to A2. On the second line , right under B1(on the "A" line) mark on the line B1-L1 and under B2 mark B2-SF. The notation "L1" refers to that this B1 story requires the completion of a special level. So you create the time line for that special level on the "B" story-line. The notation "S&F" means that the B2 story starts, and finishes at the same location. Like playing a poker challenge to get the story to unfold.

Now draw a third parallel line under the "B" line and call it "C" story-line. Then go back to your "A" line between B1 and B2, and add C1. Now you have inserted a new story to the plot. So right under "C1" on the third line mark C1-L1. And write the time-line of that special level on this third line.

You could place items that are part of the "C" story all over the place on all the story-lines. Just keep track of them by referring them as "Cx-Itemx" .

Then repeat the same methodology for the "D" story-line if you need one. "D" stories are supposed to be available to play at the players convenience so they could be anywhere on the line between "A1" and "A2".

Repeat the process between all the "A" points till you have filed you're "A" Story-line with all the events needed to build the first chapter of the game. So you have the time-line with all the events "A" to "D" for your first level on the "A" story-line, and all the details on the other lines beneath to keep track of things.

Those story-lines will become later the time-lines of the game. Those time-lines are the blue-prints of the game.

Action shooters role playing games would usually propose an "A" story unfolding with levels and a "B" story that is just being experienced as story- telling. Pretty much like a movie. But more and more games are breaking that rule by becoming a sort of an in between of RPG adventure and RPG action-shooter . The story for an action shooter role playing game must be dynamic. Be in real time. And the pace of the plot must feel like written for a movie. The quality of the story for an action shooter game will define its success, and lead to sequels.

The best way would be to perceive a good shooter RPG game, is as the media to carry a script originally designed for a movie. With the quality of texture and animations, it is in fact the direction in which the video-game industry is evolving by default. Standards of game-plays for role playing games have already been established. But more and more famous novel writers do contribution to the genre with some jewels. So if one has a good horror story, or any kind of thrilling plot to tell. It can be told with an RPG action-shooter.

The stories for strategy games are very straight forward: build, conquest, make money. The best ones are the battle strategy games; replaying very famous historic battles. They retrace sometimes the life of famous individuals.

But over the years the contents of strategy games has evolved. Strategy games are more "candy like" when they have multiple layers to their story. It is always better in a strategy game to have a main character that represents the player. Who will make bounds in the city they run. Or the army they own. A third person view is now available in strategy games. So it just calls for the input of some extra adventure and special levels with an arcade game-play.

For instance, imagine in a strategy game. Exploring ruins discovered during construction. Or disguise yourself as a civilian to fallow traitors. Even infiltrate to spy on the enemies. As the action of the genre is often battle directed, a main plot and some side stories about other things can only make the game more appealing. The story making should not take away from the quality of the game as strategy genre .But dress it with production value.

Simulation games also have a story. The most simple in the early years of gaming was : Take off the 747 in Dallas , fly it to France in real time and land in Paris. Do not crash the landing, and do not get lost at sea. That was the story for 9 hours, and we loved it.

But now the simulations offer more action than that. Best of them would react a historic event. Like a race , or a battle. For instance if it is a flight simulator about the early war-planes during the first world war. If the pilot would tilt the plane, he would see exactly how the trenches and the battle field looked in that particular battle from the historic records.

Some third person shooters are almost simulation; as they allow the player to experience an actual battle exactly as it has happened in history. And interacting with characters in the game who were there in real life. The 3D realization is from historic pictures, so the characters in the game look like the real person with their real name. These information are of domain public and often used in video games. Those type of productions always make a hit.

Plus, a good simulation game should have a good arcade mode. That allow the player to win customization for his vehicles or planes, and a collection of medals and achievements. Arcade levels must be about fun, where the pilot has to follow circle and make unbelievable acrobatic maneuvers. Or a race track that is out of this world dressed with the kind of directing you would see in an a classic "arcade" block buster.

Story-line for games on hand devices are not generally very complex. As the games for these platforms are design to offer a fast pace, game-play experience. The story-line is more dense and straight to the point. Like the early games of the 80's. Also the screen size is limited for the use of long text for the characters in a RPG to communicate.

Still; one could figure a way to have the texts slide, in an out of the screen by sliding their finger from the sides. Doing so an old school RPG in 2d, with the design of book for children, for instance, would be achievable on a hand device. As they are main sellers, one should try serving the market with those for hand devices.

Story-lines for Action-platform games are also very important for hand devices. The story of a platform game; is the whole impression received from the quality of the art directing in the graphic realization of the game. Basically the quality of the visuals and their personalization to the story's style, is the continuous story telling.

So if it is a ninja game, the whole graphic realization must be from that universe. As much as possible. Even if it must be adapted to a contemporary time . If it is a fairy tale, then the art directing of the levels and the environment must go in that direction.

The script for a comic book would be the perfect fit for a action-platform game on any console. With already a concept for the art directing. The game-play must be fluid and build with some good artistic synchronicities.

Over all, I must state again , the importance of the graphic styles and the art directing . Those two visual points are fully part of storytelling in a video game. That is pure production value.

Locations and Environments.

The environment is the world , or the maps, in which the character is going to evolve . The worlds are maps that are created by a designer in 3d, or in 2d depending on the production method.

The maps must be tailored for the game, it is the only way to do it. If it is a tank game, the maps have to be very broad , and the obstacle quit appropriate. So that the tanks can enjoy the game-play with fluidity. If it is an assassin or an infiltration game. It must have a beautiful graphic design. So that the player does not fall asleep hiding in the corners. The visuals are very important in the maps. A slow past game must have a top notch design with some real artistic inputs. Some third person shooters use real locations; that they reproduce with the perfect reflection of their beauty. It is mesmerizing when it is well done.

Changing environments is recommended for all the games. Especially for an RPG adventure. For this kind of game the map, must be quit huge. If the character where to run straight threw the map, it might take an entire hour to go from one end to the other. So to design such a universe, filled with cities and everything. The best way is to first come up with a hand drawn map of the universe you what to present. This would be the first task . Then work the details , by first putting all geographic things that the game should have. Like rivers , mountains, hills and forests. And of course the roads, all of which will get more detailed in time. Then the second task is locate your cities. The cities will often be maps that will load, when you walk in and out of them. So you will consider the design of the cities the second task. Just make a map for each city, keep in mind that they should look visually diversified.

Just like a novelist , you must get your maps more and more polished. The best would be at this point to get in contact with a very good hand drawer or sketch artist. And ask the artist to use your map prints and draw a map that looks awesome. This in fact a necessity . Because this map is your first real visual clue of what your trying to accomplish. It will also be part of the game as the map for the character in his inventory. Make the maps really net and interesting.

If the RPG is in a city; get a city map. Best a map from an old city like Chicago. A map from the 1930's. Then use that as a blue print to start geo-locating all the visual land mark and cool spots in the city. Like a nice Zoo. (There is never a nice Zoo). Or an attraction park, with a nice mini golf, and all the magnificence that these magic places should have. Make sure to have all the obvious a city needs. Like train stations, city council building, monuments, and race tracks in the outer rims. And give access to those land mark to be played in the levels and enjoyed visually. So extra production value for the game. These are things you need to focus on first. Then geo-locate all the points that are part of the story. Where the bad guy lives. The den's , and the avatar's own home.

And finally all the bar's and other spots that the game is going to need. Make should to spread all the points in the city so the character gets to explore as much as possible the city following the script of the game.

For an RPG Action/Shooter, the maps are different. The character is mainly goanna be evolving in the same direction. Basically keep walking to the end of the level. So if the level is straight it is really boring. To design a level for this shooter games, the aspect of building a little maze is a constant. Having the level start in the middle, and have the guy to explore and go all around to accomplish the level, is a better approach. For this games ; placing the secrets and the special items properly is "key" to the matter. They must be numerous and be spread to force the player to keep exploring the level, even if the way out is obvious. It adds life time to the game, and there for this details are to be considered as pure production value for a shooter game. And the quality of the textures must be of extra quality, as much as possible.

Then the variety of the different type of terrains is very important for the production value. Usually each level is a map in a different location. Like a jungle by the sea, then on mountain trails, and then the most exotic cities and such. Making the player's mind travel is a part of this type of production. Even if the game happens all in one city, the same rules apply. The producer must take the player threw a journey where he will see the most secret, and the most unbelievable places in the cities that nobody never sees.

Each location chosen, even if based on reality, must be customized for the game. The particulars of the level's game-play must be inserted specifically for each map of each level. If the player is going to come back later at the same location for a different purpose. He must experience it differently. As an example first time as a spy, the second time as a guest. And may be a third time as a prisoner. It is ok to do this repetitions, if the game-play varies every time.

And every aspect about the graphic production must be exploited to polish the maps to perfection. What the player sees in the environment; is the impression he gets from the game.

Role playing games offer a very various sets of locations, just in one game. It is in fact part of the talent to design a game, and to come up with the designs and the customization of all the maps and locations , all straight from the beginning of the concept. So the locations are somehow entirely part of the storytelling for video games. Keep this intent in mind and get creative with all the visual possibilities that could look awesome from the story itself.

Much more than in a novel, or a movie; in a video game the environment must come alive with all sorts of synchronicities and animations. The interior of the locations, must get special attention in their content. The more the setting, or the spread, of an interior is filled. The more it has an impact on the realism of the game. For instance a living room should be produced in a game, with some actual interior designs that are from a real life magazine. Plus the presence of small items on the shelves for decorations. These details carry the message for high production value.

 If the game has a particular type of fantasy genre to its story, this task becomes more difficult. Yet the same method must be applied with an adaptation to the genre. For instance if the game is happening in a universe of just fairies, and no humans. Then the visual aspects of everything in that game is goanna have to go with that palette of directing and production. So in this case; art directing is going to be most of the extra work to do. Imagine chairs and table made out of flower buds, or things like that. And it must look good and make sense.

In fact, for 2D platform games, if the whole game does not follow this rule, the game just get boring very quickly. The creation of such a universe for game-play is the first real step in to designing any video game.

Puzzle games also always present some sort of an environment where the puzzle unfolds. The more that universes is part of the puzzle the more appealing the games get. So for puzzles, the locations and the whole environment is fully part of the game-play. This is the perfect objective for adapting a puzzle to become a hit.

Creating maps for strategy games looks simple, but it is a trap. The allocation of the resources on the map and topographic conditions are part of the game-play. The key to strategy games in fact. So the whole map must be built with some sort of a chess board intention. An intention that is going to become more and more challenging at each level. This is another kind of a head ache for creating an environment. Plus in those games the cites that are build must look perfect when the player zooms in to appreciate his hard work . With all sorts of social activities. If the graphics are not appealing on that level, the game is not going to make it as best seller.

When it comes to locations it is always good in an RPG or a strategy games. To have a personalized location for the character. Like his own apartment in an RPG. Or have his own castle and real estates in a strategy game. This locations are very important as they help personalizing the character and give some emotional appeal for the player to bound with avatar.

For sports games the map is all about proportionality. The map must fit the play ground for the game. So the creativity to make them differ is very difficult. The crowd's animations and reactions are in this case a part of the environment. And the magnificence of the play ground must be complete as it is always the same location. The adaptation of sports game could be interesting because they naturally offer a setting for advertisement.

In car games the environments are obviously the race tracks. In simulations ; what you see in real tracks, is exactly what you get in the games. Up to the track itself being original in proportions. It gets as simple as that , for car and sports simulations.

For car games set in an urban environment. The best is to use the same proportionalities as actual real famous cities. It always adds immensely to the production value of the game. If the game could have land mark commerce, and businesses exactly where they are in real existence; that would really cut it.

And with the presence of an arcade mode everything is possible. Having an arcade mode within this games that provides some really surreal circuits is a very nice touch. It is always fun to race with a custom car, somehow by jumping from roof to roof. This kind of approach is often missing in most car games.

The quality of the sky and the sun's reflections are very important to be optimized in a car game's environment. The different light for the different hours of the day, and the realism of the reflection's on the road are straightly related as environment factors for all car games. Argo, production value. The urban car racing game must offer a smart map . In the sense that not only the proportions must be right for racing in the city. But also offer numerous kinds of locations to race. From racing in sewers, to racing on a beach. So the city map must be filled with good looking land marks for the visuals of the races.

For smaller devices all types of environments must be designed so that the player can see easily what is represented on the screen. Particularly for smart phones. So for this devices the environment is always scrolling in the direction in which the character is going. The best would be a map designed in 2D, quit similar to the ones for strategy games. One giant map, with the right positioning of everything that the level needs. And the character starts evolving in this map as a game level. Always seen from an upper view straight to the ground. Or may be some times a little tilted. This method can allow the creation of an elaborate role playing games . If the memory of the hard ware on the device can take it. But we will discuss this later with more detail.

Creating your Maps

To make a first representation of your playable maps, you will need to get some very large white paper boards. And draw a print of the level maps for at least one level of the game. If it is a strategy game or so ; the map must look like a geographic map. With topographic elements to it.

If the game is an adventure RPG, you make a map of the whole universe with all the details you can. And also a map of the first city, and some of its exterior beyond the walls. And In this two cases, make the maps from an up view , like a treasure map.

For shooters and platform games, the map is going to be a simple sort of maze. Make sure that the parallel lines to make the maze are quit spaced from each other. As you will need to insert notes on story and action game-play as you go further in the project.

Ounce you have your maps; then you will progressively insert all the points from the time-lines in to the map with, pointers and notes. The team is going to need a method to make annotations and name the pieces of the project. The best way is to keep it simple like computer C++ language.

It is also very important to make sure to size this project properly so you don't run out of room. For the better generation; using a computer is recommended if possible. This maps will change, over and over again, and get filled with all the information that you have in the time-lines. So the last draws must look very pro, and intelligible. Because they will also be part of the packaging to get financing.

Time-lines & Planning Process

Basically when you start adding to the story-lines the details of the individual levels and all the notes for the game-play, the story-lines become time-lines. So you must make sure that the story plot is well proportion for each level of the time-lines. With all different type of "A" to "D" story plots. The work on these schematics are very important; so keep the time-lines updated as you go.

Platform games are really net for small devices. To map a platform game, the best is to start with a simple hand drawn design of each level . But look at it like a time-line. A time-line that you will progressively fill with all the platforms. Then on the second pass, you polish to insert different paths through the platforms . Then you make another pass to insert secrets levels, or hidden goodies. You keep making passes from the beginning of the level to the end . And keep zooming in the details, till you have all you need. Where you need it happening. The last point to cover would be some screen animations, like rain, reflection, nice colors plays and other add-ons as such.

To resume; you will first need for any game a first time-line, divided by the chapters (or levels). Then start adding the initial contents, like level-bosses and the essentials of the game-play. Progressively keep adding all the details, in regard to every chapter.

As an example draw a straight line, and put a notch, write in a parentheses 5 enemy in lobby. Then a little bit further put another notch. And write in parentheses Booby trap in elevator on the way up. And so on, to invent the game-play. Remember also all the animations in the environment. Like all the back ground events to garnish the level. Mention in the annotations the different locations that will fallow each other, and the details about their specific "looks". Just insert details in the time-line so the story line gets some life.

At this point the story-lines, have become fully loaded time-lines. All story-lines from "A" to "D" should come alive with a full dressing of all they need. To keep track of thing more simply make also a main time-line with all the main events in their proper sequence. This will helps to keep track of where you stand later in your production process.

Then you would have to repeat this process for every level individually. And make passes over the lines, over and over, to garnish them with the proper content. Fallowing this process the levels contents and environment will be almost completely visualized and ready to be produced for the whole game. (Good work). In addition the use of a fourth line in the bottom just to take annotations of all the environmental essentials and the save points is recommended.

The creation of the story-lines , that will become the time-lines, is the journal of the producer. Those are the files the most close to him. Every time that an idea or a change must be added; the first place to put it is in the appropriate time-line. Exactly like a music partition the producer can see all the events like a rhythm that he can control by placing all the events appropriately. Making sure than all the events in the stories are enveloped with proper production value.

Those time-lines are goanna be written and re-written again. If you start getting lost in the notes; it is good sign . Just make sure to keep track of the abbreviations that you will use on the time-lines; and make sure to write them vertically to the lines.

This method of time-line to organize the game can be used for all the games; you just adapt the logic to the different variations. Eventually some time-lines will come together mixed in one big time line. With two different colors for each category of events on the same line. The producer is goanna have to do this work to adapt; the time-lines progressively as the project gets deeper. The time-lines are the only way to explain the idea and the structuring of the game to the team. So a sense of logic must come from it.

As an example for a strategy game, with only one "A" story and there for, "B" side stories. The original two story-lines made to organize the plot adaptation, are going to be used as original time-lines. So , as an example, the first line for the "A" story for the first level would start with :

-First mark: Story A1-an01(the first thing the animation to present the character and the story: an01.)

-Second mark: Start building settlements.

-Third to Fifth mark: Add events that challenge the player while he builds the city.(attacks, running out of space, explore .....)

-Sixth mark: B1-01 Character walks up to the player and gives quest. At this point, the B1-L1 should be inserted on the second line, beneath the "A" line, right under B1-01. Because that new Location(B1-L1) where the player is going to have to go is now available. And will have a time-line of its own to be marked on that "B" line. The B1-L1 could be a third view level to explore a cave with its own little details to be added on the "B" line to complete that specific independent Level.

-Back to the first line, insert seventh mark: The city changes to level two of evolution.

This is an example of how a story-lines can blend with a time-line for a the strategy game. And as the producer review them he can progressively add all the details up to animations and game-play events. So each line should end up with one type of events on it. And all the other details discussed earlier.

To make a time-line for a puzzle with a little story, you would essentially need one line. As an example, the story is more the puzzle unfolds, the more a rock climber gets momentum in the back ground to get to the top of the mountain. So on your time-line would be:

-First mark: Presentation screen of the puzzle with representation of the climber.

-Second mark: Menu to chose the game mode and options.

-Third mark: Get ready screen before the game starts .

-Fourth mark: When climber reaches a certain level make challenge faster.

And so on, till the guy makes it to the top of the mountain.

For RPG's you will have to use at least five lines, one for each story , plus one for additional material that are just goanna be necessary as the game is being build. Like game engine routines for the programmer later.

For a car game the time-lines are going to be about three. the first line , for the races, the second line for the street challenges, and the third line all the environmental animations. Because a car game is all about visuals. So the third line is the most important. Just insert cool things to see.

The implementation of the time-lines is of the out most importance. For the communication of the production process and later to get some financing. Keep that in mind ,make sure they look very pro.

Imagination And Logic At Work

At this point the reader should have a better understanding of all the details that he needs to get his head around to have an entire game concept. The best is to start playing with time-lines, and the maps.

Now the work is about imagination, and adaptation. Either you have just a game-play but no story. Or a story but no game-play. Anyway, the next step is where it must all come to one in good story; good game-play. An action based story is often necessary to carry a video game. But the action could carry a side story that is pure horror drama. The kind of drama that inspires Hollywood movies to be made from video games.

Video games are also a visual media, so it is all about the "looks" . The kind of visual presentation that you want for the game is a very important decision. Take time to choose if your project is better looking contemporary, or it is better as a fantasy science fiction. Make your pick wisely, thinking about the better visuals.

Then start imagining an artistic style of graphics that is peculiar to the game. The choice of the look does not need to be compatible with the story . This is what it means imagination and logic at work.

A story could be adapted to any kind of look. For example ,a cop movie could become the same plot, but assigned to two centurions, inquiring a mysterious murder during the age of Rome. With side stories about ancient demonic religions .The whole plot happening as a side story in a strategy game. Where, the game-play changes by shifting to a first-person view, so the player can pursues this dire quest's, all as a RPG game in a strategy game.

The side stories could also have more of a forensic and puzzling kind of game-play, using labs and benches to study the clues collected. The more this "B", "C" and "D" stories offer surprising missions, the better the game. Giving missions of a social aspect are getting more and more popular. Missions that are only directed to the story drama. Basically the player is going to have to be the "Cool" human that will help the situation. Perfect hero versus anti-hero duality for the player to identify through the avatar. Being a bad guy but doing good deeds.

As other example imagine that all the clues collected in a platform game, become the pieces of a tragic conspiracy. Or even better, a love story. If the player misses the clues he misses the story. The story can be an awesome animation with sensual presentations so the player is inclines to play the levels till he get all the clues to see the full side stories. In this case that would be production value as it adds to the amounts of hours to play to finish the game.

So over all , make sure to take precise notes of all your thinking. If you want to make a game; probably at this point of the reading; you have a good impression of what you want. But it is brainstorming in your mind and you don't know where to begin.

This is a simple method to start organically building your game when you have the story in mind. As an example, let's say that we are working on a adventure RPG's with a "A" to "D" story.

Now just take a piece of blank paper, and draw a straight line. Then insert notes "A1" to "A3" all equidistant from each other. You have your first basic time-line for the first level.

Between "A1" and "A2" Insert "B1-01" and "B1-02". In this case the player has to complete two different "B" stories to get to "A2". As soon as these "B" stories are given their locations B1-L01 is noted to the second time-line and implemented as it should for that specific level.

Now between "A1" and "B1-01" , insert "SecretC1-I1". So the player is supposed to find the first item related to the "C1" story. An item that he will just keep till he understands its use.

Now between "B1-01" and "B2-02" , insert "C1". The player is going to meet a man at the market who will explain the nature of the item he has found earlier. And clues where to go next for more information. Like the location of a secret cave. Call it already "C1-L1" place it right before "A2".

Now You must take some time garnishing the game with visuals. So insert right after "A1" , an animation annotation Add a note about a beautiful giant tree right at the beginning of the level. With extra wind animations and birds living on it. Extra textures and extra light work and shading.

Then right after "B1-01", insert a note about a beautiful windmill. Then insert right next to the windmill note "D1-I1". The player can find a secret location with a secret item exploring around the windmill. Like a strange doll.

Now to add some action and drama. "A2" is an animations of the town being attacked. Go between "A2" and "A3". Insert town attack, protect the town. Then add "D1","D2" then "D3". The town is going to be rampaged by enemies, and you must kill them all. In that process at "D1", is a point where you must get a girl out of a burning house. And she won't move till you show her the doll you found by the wind mile. And at "D2" you must heal the husband of a women who is dying by using your medi-kit. In between "D1" and "D2" insert "B3". A level where the avatar must get in a building and kill the general using the "C1-I01". So the third animation of the level "A3" on the story is preceded with some drama

Voila! Now you zoom in between all the points, and add more visual animations and game action, whatever you need to make the game awesome. It is important to insert as many as environmental visual goodies as you can. So you might want to use a second line under the first when you are brainstorming, just to put notes of the visual add-ons. Make sure to insert them also inside the side levels.

Ounce your are satisfied with your "draft time-line" , then you put it down properly by separating all the events and placing them on their own appropriate time-line, and make sure to keep the placement of the insertions all in order. Just looking at your project on a proper lining, should give you more ideas about the blanks to garnish on each time-line.

Let's make another example for a build and conquest strategy game using the story of the two centurions. In this type of game, it is the level of the constructions that is pacing the level. In this example let's say that the cities have 3 levels of evolution to complete for the level to end.

So draw a draft time-line and place three marks equidistant from each other. And call them CityLevel01, then CityLeve02 and finally City Level03. (Or CiLv01,CiLv02 and CiLv03).And We will refer as "A" story everything that relates to the towns and the strategic game-play. And "B" all the story related to the actual demonic plot.

Now on the line right after CiLv01 , mark "A1". A1 is an animation scene of the people coming on the grounds and the main character giving orders to settle and look for resources.

Then on the time-line after A1, mark B1. During constructions, they have found ruins, with a secret tomb. Big drama workers died in traps. So now there is special level to explore with a RPG type of game-play. Right next to B1 mark in parenthesis "B1-I1". In that special level the character is going to find an magic artifact .Later polishing the time-lines, B1-I1, will be displaced on the second "B" time-line, where the special level is outlined.

Then on the line right after "B1-L1" mark "B2". The town is going to be attacked by a magic golem of stone. After he is defeated it reveals that his presence was related to the discovery of the artifact.

Then right after "B2" mark "A2". The town has reached a level of prosperity fair enough for travelers to come and do commerce. It is time to spend money on entertainment and touristic structures, as bar and hotels and so.

Then right after "A2" mark "A3" , the town is experiencing a drought and the neighboring hords are looting the city. Time to spend money on the city infrastructure and rural construction to keep the town safe and wealthy.

Then right after "A3" , mark "B3". A tourist In the city (always evolving); has been found butchered in his hotel with strange demonic tags on the walls. Bad for commerce, numbers are going down. The main character must go personally to investigate the crime premises. Right next to "B3" mark "B3-l01". During the investigation the avatar will find two clues. A particular type of sign on the wall, and a burned piece of paper with half a sentence on it in.

Now right after "B3" and "B3-l01" mark A4. The town is attacked this time by demonic wolfs that are all over the city. Ounce they are killed their demonic heart and skin sells for very good money , so the city can jump into level 2.

Right after CiLv02 mark on the line "A5", it is time to go explore the map much further to find new mines and other resources.

Then right after "A5" mark "B4". Some ruin are found with the same demonic marking as in the murder scene. The news is intriguing so the character must now go there personally. In this case the marking on the ruins match the clue of the tag and form a map indicating a secret mine entrance .

Then on the time-line insert "A6", the character and his army get attacked by a legion of zombies discovering the secret mine. And the city gets attacked by barbarian from the south at the same time.(better to have build some defenses and left a good army reserve behind, or end-game.)

Now mark "B5" right after "A6" on the time-line. They found the mine with some nice resources around to start a new little settlement. And the character can go in the mine while the settlements are starting. After slaying some more terrible zombies, deep in the mine. Observing a small dolmen the character will use the clues on the paper to decipher a puzzle. That will open a secret compartment with an ancient magic book hidden in it.

Now after "B5" mark "A7". There is a sudden curse on the land; the harvest is compromised and the cattle are dying. Time to get smart with commerce and trade to balance things out.

After "A7" mark "B6", the main character finds a scholar in the academy (that he can finally build) to translate the book ; understand its history and a spell to bless the land and make it fertile again. To do so he will need more resources to build a particular structure for the ceremony. So the main character will have to send scouts to explore the land further and create new settlements with extra protection for the more and more extending routes. And also keep an eye on commerce.

After "B6" mark "A8", there is a small revolt in town concerning the leader ship and the intentions of the main character to have a demonic ceremony. Numbers are plummeting. So the character is going to have to play his political skills (tax reform) and build more temples to reassure the people.

Now mark "B7" right after "A8". The structure is finally build and the ceremony is performed. With some revelations about the true nature of the history of the region, the land is healed. Commerce is booming. So the town is ready is jump to its last level "CiLv03".

Right after "CiLv03", mark B8 . People from the east have come to ask assistance to the town because of strange things that have happened since they have found another artifact. The character is going to have to go there with an army and save the town. And also get the artifact.

Now after "B8" Mark "A9". Back to town, in the academy the mage has put the artifacts together and using the book he has accidentally open a door way from which the army of darkness are encircling the town to get the artifacts . This is the last stand of the level. After the battle is completed , insert a good animation to prepare for the next level and its plot.

To make the work more acute, the creator now should just draw three parallel lines and put in the first-time-line("A" story) all the City "related" events and also all the visual components regarding that particular angle of the game. On the second line place all the points related to the demonic side story. On this "B" time-line, then create the outline for those RPG levels. And add all the visual goodies that you need to garnish around these "B" levels and happenings.

 Use the third line to add even more back ground animations everywhere in the level. And also mark points where new mines and resources are going to be available. Use the third line for all the technical stuff the city needs to grow.

Once you get the hang of this .This brainstorming method on a time-line becomes loads of fun and the project will come together very quickly.

The imagination work is everything. If one is trying to make a sports game for instance. As they are licensed, and only accessible to the big boys of the industry. The creator must come up with a whole new approach to the environment. He must somehow add stories, and imagine a entire look for everything. But keep the rules and the setting of the sport as they are. And if those are protected by rights ; then change the proportions and adapt the game-play, to make it better than the real thing. This approach to sports was the rage in the early ages of the gaming industry. With all types of fantasy sports games, all based on real sport with the same rules. This approach of awesome sports adaptations is still a very good angle for today.

For puzzles , the imagination and the logic at work are going to come together as one epic and blinding head ach. (Relax, that is how it works). To remake a pre-existing standard puzzles ,the work is all about imagination . Coming up with a way to have a story that will use the environment to become part of the puzzle is gold. This could take time but if it accomplished properly it will probably become a best seller. That is a nice trade off for the headaches. If one can come up with a whole new concept, for a puzzle that is the joy. That person will be establishing a new standard and make big bucks.

This very particular creative process is the same either you are designing for a console, or a hand device. This first early steps are the same, so make sure to use your creativity with its maximum output. Put all that you can think of, that is good, in the concept. So when trimmed down for the last version; it looks perfect and reflects high production value.

Chapter2

Art Directing & Creative Process

To Do List:

-Get on line using social medias to find a sound engineer and a 3D animator. Build up your team. Understand yours needs as you go.

-Pick an art directing style for your game. Take time to ponder on this decision to get creative with the team.

-Spend time working on your characters and their respective drawings and representations.

-Start working on some wallpaper art projects for the game. Expose them on the blogs. Get feedback.

-Start keeping track and make lists of additional tasks to accomplish for production. Keep taking notes of new ideas.

-Organize the task lists to direct the production line in order to get a tetra demo for the first level ASAP.

-Take the work on the color-palette as seriously as possible.

-Make sure to vary palettes in regard of locations.

-Start designing the locations and environments.

-Start working on your game-play and - inserting all the needed material for the game on the time-lines.

-Start working on the sounds and music. Animations for the tetra demo.

-Keep the blog about the game updated with the material.

-Get exposure on internet sites that helps with financing projects by reaching to - "individual Cloud investors". Keep the material exposed updated.

-Fallow the feedback that you will get from people on the blogs and so. Always listen for good tips.

-Make your team tight and happy.

Art Directing & Creative Process

The following about art directing, is the same process for either consoles or hand devices. Do not think that because it is a hand device; it will not require all the attention as detailed below. The more work on art directing the more production value for hand devices, and consoles alike.

Characters & Items Creation.

If you have a story with characters, you are going to need very high quality; hand drawn pictures, of everyone of them. The use of a good professional drawer is again recommended as the use of this drawings will be very important to communicate the concept, and will be part of the packaging.

Each drawing must be the size of the whole page, So that the eye can clearly see all the details of the characters. Present the characters with all the attributes that the story gives them. That would be specific physical looks, clothes; but also close items from the universe of the game. It must be present in those drawings. Like the main characters guns or his sword. Produce drawings for each character of the game, enemies and animals included; with all attributes from both the story and the game-play.

Then you will need a second drawing, of all your characters with a different aspect.

Three full body drawings; a facial , lateral and back drawing, of the same character on the same page. All three of the same dimensions with arms lifted to shoulders. These drawings should be made on millimeter paper. So the dimension of the characters are all ready to be measured for the 3D artist to produce them in mesh.

For car games, The same is going to be required. Two drawings of all the cars, with different customizations. Plus drawings of the people who are part of the crowd, and all other animated objects of the game. The point of drawing a car is all about the customization that you bring to the paint job, those are the aspects that need to be emphasized in the drawings. But drawing of other animated objects in the crowd must also be of great variety so the game is not repetitive.

For puzzle games, the drawings must be all about the "bling" that the screen is goanna have when the puzzle is running. So basically make a nice drawn representation, on a full page, of what the screen is going to look like. Plus drawing of all the pieces of the puzzle, on a millimeter paper with the proper coloring. The first wallpaper that is presented for introduction in a puzzle video game is crucial for the games production value. So in this particular case it must look awesome.

Strategy games , have numerous aspect here for the conceptualization . The number of standalone items and structures is what the game is about. So in this case you will need to produce a drawing of the most important structures that are part of the game. For instance a watch tower or the command center. In strategy games, the level of this structures increases with the game. So they have four to five different aspect , one for each time they jump a level.

A drawing of this buildings that shows they progressive change in looks, all in one page is the objective. Each drawing must be large, and present clearly the details of the structures. In a strategy game this pieces of structure are the game. The hand drawing of this buildings must be impressive, with as much detail as you can put in it. So you must spend time communicating with the drawer about this aspects.

Strategy games are also full of characters. As workers, soldiers, citizens, and a lot more for fantasy games. Every single one of the little guys must be hand drawn properly in a large size. And expose clearly in which aspect they are different from one another in regard of their social class.

Drawings of the war vehicles, and flying crafts must also have the proper intention as they carry the genre of the game. Everything that is goanna be on the screen of the game must have a visual representation drawn. The large variety of these items and characters is the production value of the game . So you should end up with a lot of drawings for a strategy game. And it would be a very good sign.

If the strategy game has a story with characters. Then as we discussed in the beginning, a nice representation of each of them is goanna be needed. Plus a drawing of their habitat. As their house or their castle. In a strategy game, characters are often related to specific locations. So it is better to represent it in the early concept. Also add some extra characters in the design for commerce. So if the camera zooms in for those sequences the characters in the shops are net, and vary in appearance as much as possible.

For RPGs of any kind. The items and the gears are to be really good looking, as all the objects in a 3D RPG must look real. So the use of on-line 3D models libraries could be very practical. Just make sure to keep track of all the items you need for this large type of games.

For any game as you create these first aspects to visualize your concept. You are also better of producing some of the other materials that are goanna be present in the game. Like objects and furniture. Especially if you are making any game that is out of time and space. Even in a Role playing game if the character lives in a particular environment, you must be able to represent that with actual drawings.

Working on these drawings with your artist is the first step of your art directing. This is the point where the visual genre of your game is going to be invented. If it is a science fiction, then the aspect of that future and aliens are goanna be invented from this point on. The last result on the screen will be consequence of your choices here as art director.

So it is important to take time to really anchor in your mind what kind of artistic approach you want. And if you are not making the drawings yourself, you must be able to communicate with your first team mate properly to get it right.

For additional notes on character creation. There is some sort of a rule to follow if the game is a RPG adventure or shooter. Like any good action movie the main character is presented to be perceived as going through hell and keep pushing; because he cares. And the ending of the movie can then vary as it goes.

In a video game , the character must be immediately presented with a full past history. A past that he hates and feels guilty about. And he goes through hell not only because he cares, but also because it sizzles his addiction to the past sins. And the most important reason why he is doing all of this; is to seek the truth. A revelation that will transform the character for the better forever. This is the ultimate endings for vide-games.

A transformation for the better if the player chose one ending. Or a dark revelation if the player chooses the other path. And sometimes a third path the "weird" way in some games.

It is almost a rule to have these dynamics synchronized in the game. Those are the aspect that make the player bound to the avatar. Those are the types of adaptations that you need to transit a character from a novel to a video game; and keep carrying the note with the graphical art directing.

Color palette and Ambiance.

At this point the producer should have gathered:

A nice map of the universe for the game.

A good story; scripted by chapters for the different levels.

The story scripted in "A" to "D" story-lines. (if your story is elaborate).Sequenced properly for each chapter.

A full grip of the game genre and game-play. Plus an understanding of the adaptations needed for the story.

A general time-line for the entire game divided by the chapters, for main exposition of the game to the artists. Plus a detailed time-lines for one or two additional levels.

A mapping of one entire level, with the technical inputs for the game action and story points. And of proper size for exposition.

A whole bunch of polished and detailed drawings about all that you need to present in the game. With the actual measurements ready to be collected from the millimeter papers.

Now you are going to need a new friend. It is time to make buds with a 3D designer. And the first step, is all three team mates in a room composing the color palettes.

To make the game professionally you are going to need your artist to create a color palette. It is a process of toning colors so they blend within each other properly. For Gaming it is very important to pay attention to this detail. It will really reflect in the quality of your graphics at all levels.

The color palette must have one main toning. Then be adapted to the locations with a different spectrum of diffusion to make the change effects for the ambiance . This is a technical and crucial need. Using a composed color palette for the early concept drawings is also the best way to go.

To intensify the quality of the different ambiances in the game. From different exteriors to different interiors, it might be need to create a custom color palette (in derivative of the initial) for each case. It adds to the "ambiance" value. It is crucial to use this method to contrast the environment in the game map. And also to contrast the decoration of an interior from the structure itself. So the objects don't look like they are glued to the shelves and the walls.

Also make sure to give the main character a brighter palette, and the bad guy a darker one. This understanding of the use of color palettes to "ambiance" the game, is directly related to the final production value.

For car games the work on color palettes is about everything. As the animation is just about shifts in the color palettes to give an impression of momentum to the car. In this case the palette is part of the animation in a full gear.

Sports game must have a appealing color palette. Just like for a good advertisement . The blush of the color must carry that sense of commercial environment. (Even for the fantasy genre).

For strategy games the color palette must be large. It is going to take a lot of coloring for the details of a universe in a big game. As the representations are small on the screen, the palette must be optimized for that view. To make the pixelisation optimal. And show a clear difference for each different types of terrain, and the space between things.

Puzzle and casino games must have an "eye candy" blush to their color palette. (Like using actual candy colors it is very smart.) The color palette has to be quite large, more than expected, because it is better to keep the same palette for the entire game.

 The use of a brighter secondary palette just for the shinny events and animations of the puzzles is in fact the only way to go ,as they are the only animation the game could have. So the palette is the ambiance for this category. Argo, pure production value. It would be 50 percent of the art directing.

Back grounds

Now the 3D artist can start making the meshes and use colors to create some of the 3D models. And so the producer and the artist can focus on the following.

The back grounds are images that are the line of horizon in the game. If the location is in a jungle, the background picture would be a jungle. It sounds simple, but it must be entirely exploited as art directing drama.

The creation of back grounds and environments for video games, is the most of the work to be done for their creation. Back grounds and environment are closely entangled for the design of a video-game. Most of the time they are the same thing, and they carry the plot in there content.

For a puzzle, in the most simple cases, the back ground would be an image where the puzzle is simply exposed. Like a wall paper on a desktop. But the use of a back ground in a puzzle game must have much more originality than just that. Simple animations of galaxies and other very geometrical back grounds are more in vogue.

All puzzle back grounds are essentially animations, they will change with the increasing level of the puzzle. The more the level increases the more the back ground's animations gets funky and accentuated. It is important to spend extra time designing the back ground for a puzzle, there is no straight method, just use your imagination and make it look top graphically.

For a strategy game , the back ground is essentially the quality of the nature and the terrain. Even from a far view it must look really awesome or the game is not really goanna hit the market. The color palette must show the nature and the terrain a bit like poping out of the screen, in contrast to the building structures. And menus are to be include here as back grounds because they are going to be open and close every five seconds. So their conception is very crucial to the game and to be considered as production value.

For car games, the back ground is the map, the horizon point, and the sky. In car games the different back grounds are to be considered as part of the game's action and game-play. The horizon line must be on spin . So when the car turn form on direction to the other, the horizon line offers a different view.

The map is the race tracks and the streets, they must have an appropriate color palette and realization. If the cities and tracks don't look easy for the eye with great variety. The game is goanna be a fail. So the use of quality textures for the mapping is an absolute "must" for car games. And each buildings should have a slightly different texture to it, to add to the speed sensation.

And obviously there must be an extra effort for the texture of the roads. As they change, they must have the best textures in the game. They have priority over the other textures.

The sky ,as a back ground, is a composition of a back ground wallpaper and animations of lights and clouds. Even birds and plane and weather events. The light from the sky and the way it reflects and shadows on the map is a direct effect on the speed sensation of the game. So the back ground lights diffusion and reflections, is part of the game-play. There for in a car game the back grounds and environment melt together.

For platform games on hand devices or console alike. The back ground is a direct representation of an environment that unfolds as the player moves left of right. Like the interior of a building floor. So the quality of the representations and the complexity of the back grounds details, are locating the character in the story line. So the locations must be numerous and yet also tell the story of the game in their drawings. This is true for all games but it is in emphasis for this type of games.

So for platform game's, the back ground is part of the story-lines, as it cadences the game-play time-line. Basically the back grounds for a platform game should come together at the time-lining of the game as we discussed earlier. By the process of polishing ,over and over, till it is all in place.

In platform games back grounds are 85 percent of the production value of the whole game. As they are the play map, the locations and the environment all at the same time. Plus they must carry the story.

For RPG's the back ground is a composition of different effects and material representations. It is basically everything that the camera is showing on the screen. Variety is therefore everything for an RPG's immediate back ground. This means more work for the drawer to produce different types of drawings of the same things. Like trees , benches, you name it. Expose them all on the same paper if possible, organized by type. The good news is that you won't need a millimeter drawing for most of this items. The 3D designer will make it happen.

Make at least four to five different types of trees and flowers and field terrains. At least ten different types of interior designs . With as much as possible decorative stuff for those interiors.

Make also a maximum of drawings of the scenery; as buildings and commerce. That are there in the game but not part of the game-play. So it will require the creation of a whole "look" for the streets . The art directing of this details must be done with time and consideration.

Also put notes on the drawings of environmental effects. As weather effects and people working in the back grounds and other things to bring the game alive. As these will require later some animation work you must set them now, and be generous because they bring the environment to life for RPG gaming. Make this work as fully as possible. It is pure production value at the end. Progressively bring your drawings and models to your 3D designer and give him all the tools he needs to keep the job going.

Game-play "immediate" environment

If you have gathered so far enough material. Then you should be able to start working on your "tetra demo" and get a good impression of your game-play environment. The tetra demo is the realization of the game on screen for a first viewing of what it 's going to look like. And if the play ground is fun to experience in the game. So you should insert on the level maps all that is needed for game-play purpose.

If it is a puzzle game the tetra demo should have all the layouts of the puzzle and all the pieces of the puzzles in the layout. Also show all the back ground and the eventual environment fully with good detail.

This demo , at this level must allow to see the pieces in motion and also allow the interaction of the tester to move the pieces. This is all about a first proper test to see if the game-play is fluid and the commands are responsive. The tester must be able to see if moving the pieces as needed, fits properly with fluidity for the game-play. No slowdowns and such.

For a strategy game , you can now put in the computer all the material necessary to build a city to at least level two. The point here in a tetra demo, is to see if the contrasting of the nature and the buildings are pretty enough. Basically, observing the color palettes working all in one. To see if it is working for the pleasure of the eye. A 2D, (or better a 3d) animation of the little guys coming and settling, then growing the city is what you need here. An straight animation of how the game-plays would look like, with the menus opening and closing to see if their styling is fitting the game.

The tester must be able to move the camera at will; and see if the game looks appropriate. The demo must also give an example of the different camera effects that are goanna be used on the play map. Plus some weathering effects.

For sports games, the tetra demo should show an animation of a full game where ,you kick back and watch. It is all about camera movements and zooms. The point of the tetra demo in a sports game is to show the quality of the color palette, and the quality of the camera management and the impression of speed.

So get your first tetra demo started with the material you have. (A well polished "Tetra" demo could be considered as a proper demo to make a presentation for sale. With the quality of all the material that is drawn. Plus the intelligibility of the game's planning layouts and files.)

But there is still some work to do before completing a full beta demo. To polish the game-play's immediate environment. It is time to start inserting in the game's level maps all the details directly related to game-play. The save points , also all the gear to pick up and enemies locations; also secrets and other things. All the stuff that the character is goanna have to interact with. If in his path there is some sort of a puzzle to open the tracks, they must also be set in the level map with precision. The insertion of all environmental effects must also be included in this part. Remember to be generous and create custom scenery views for each part of the game.

For Role playing games, at this point it is time to make sure that the maps, with all the details "inserted" as the environment and with all the necessary back ground effects, gives enough room for the game-play to be fluid. (A second draft of your original level map is ready to be under taken). Have the characters play grounds perfected with creativity and "bling".

So at this point you must go through the levels on paper, (or in 3D if you have them) ;to make sure that everybody has room to maneuver. And check if the proportionality of the buildings are fit. So you don't feel like the characters are little persons. Then make sure to add all that you need to make the game fun; like points for cover, and all that you need for the action of the game.

As a new set of inputs, in this process you will start inserting elements of the actual game-play environment. That is everything that the character can play with, animate and non-animated. All this material must come together so that the game is proportional and logical.

For a car game the game-play environment is all the things that the car can crash in. Or the locations he can drive into. Locations for hiding, ware houses, or to start races and story points. All of this locations must be now represented on the map with a spread that is logical. But most of the work is going to be all the little things that the car can displace and destroy with great variety. Especially if it is a city based game.

 Also insert all the notes for environment animations, and also the points where they are goanna be special reflection effects, in the city, on the tracks, and also in nature. To make sure the game is pretty, the best way is to insert manually a lot special effects of pure awesomeness in sightseeing, all over the place, for all type of games.

During this process numerous aspects a lot of the many animations that you are going to need are just goanna reveal themselves. Very simple cases of just opening and closing doors and also more complex cases with social interactions. All new details will be revealed as animations. Make sure to take note of them and make a list of the animation needed as they will present themselves.

Inventory and Items

All inventory and menu designs are pure production value. For all the different type of games. The fallowing is to be emphasized as much as any other point during the production.

Most genres have items that are part of the game and that will display in a menu. It is very important that all the items look absolutely gorgeous in the inventory. If the player is presented the items in a very small format in the inventory they must look all "eye candy". The designers and the art director must now spend time polishing the items that the characters are going to have to interact with. I cannot stress enough the importance of their "looks". At this point in the project this should be the last draw about these items. In 2d and in 3d.

The inventory lay out must be appropriate to the game genre. For a puzzles , the inventory is essentially going to be about the games settings and different modes. Usually to have options in the menu to change and personalize a bit the back grounds is much appreciated from players. Overall the menu must be customized to the art of the game and be simple in its executions.

For strategy games the menu and inventories are full part of the game-play. They must really fit the art directing of the game. If it is a dungeon and dragons games, the inventory and menu should un-scroll like parchments. If it is a science fiction game then the menu must look like a super computer screen. The creation of the menus must be fit and simple for their adaptations, but look really net with their colors and fonts.

The menus for strategy games get very complex. It is there for crucial that they are intelligible and make sense in their sequencing. So the production of the menus and there design is a whole task of its own. For a valid strategy game. If the game has a main character leading the story it is recommended that the avatar would have a more personalized design for his particular inventory and skills menu. So to accentuate the impression of having two different type of game play in the game.(But the player should be able to open both at the same time on the screen if he wishes.)

For sports games the menu is to be designed looking like the panels that they use on TV to expose information on the screen during the game. The game's menus should have the same layout type of designs and art directing. It is very important because it is what will add to the ambiance of the game. For some sports , the menu can get as complex as a for strategy games. So it must be clear and logical in it sequencing.

For car games, the menu is to be looking like a mix between blue-prints for car engineering and a super computer. Everything to dive in the world of cars and mechanics. Usually with cars exposed in the back ground spinning with a 3D effect. The items in the inventories must represent some of the professional aspect to them. The other menus should only be available in regards to the location of the driver. So each location that the driver is going to drive in for the purpose of game-play, is going to have the a specific look for the menu about that place.

For RPG action games a menu must propose the different adaptations that the player wants to make to the avatars skills and gear. The menu in between levels must not be to complex, yet blend perfectly with that art directing of the game. The main menu must pause the game and show a clear list of the options.

For RPG's , The main menu is usually all the technical part about settings and so. But the essential menu of the game is going to be the personal inventory and the inventory presentations for commerce. And also the inventory/menu for the labs and work benches. So in this case of labs or special environments the menus must have a very artistic aspect to it.

Or at least make sure that the main map is represented like a real map on paper, it gives a sense of reality to the ambiance. The items in the inventory must be represented in 3D, full size, with all their awesomeness.

If the player clicks on one of items it should zoom out in 3D, and look magnificent. If the RPG is set in a fantasy environment.

Then it is important to have all the graphics representations of the upgrades on weaponry and shielding. They should be clearly visible when the weapons are exposed in the inventory.

Sounds & Music

The creation of sounds and music for a video-game is a production aspect that is as important as the graphic art directing. The trick; is to understand that every action in the game must have a sound to bring it to life. In this process, two task will be accomplished in one. The listing of the sounds, and the listing of all the animation's details. We will build them at the same time. So they become one piece of the game's blue-print.

So far in the creation task; a lot of small animations necessities must have revealed their logical need. As crash sounds, explosion, cats and dogs, what have you. All of that in addition to the eventual voices for characters, and menu sounds. Your job is to have a full list of all of this essential animations. This should be quite a large list. Basically, for now, every time that you need a sound effect in the game you just account it as an animation. Even if it is just the music.

The best method to organize and keep track of all this work. Is to make a series of specific lists. The first list call it Animations Environment Essentials .

As example:

-AnEnEs-001: sound of street/back ground/ Always on: AnEnEsSound001(the name of specific sound file).

-AnEnEs-002: sound of cars/back ground/ On-Off(the sounds must start when cars drive by, then stop)./SoundAnEnEs002

This a good example of how to organize your files. The second list is about Game-play. Call it Animation Game-Play Essentials. For example :

-AnGpEs-001 : Sound of character's footsteps walking/ For ground (loud and clear)/On-Off/ SoundAnGpEs001.

-AnGpEs-002 : Sound of character's footsteps sprinting/For Ground/On-Off/SoundAnGpEs-002

The third list call it Animation Action-Reaction Essentials. All the effects as bullet impacts or the sound of explosion and crashes. Everything that is a reaction to the actions happening in the game. As example:

-AnAcReEs-001/Rocks rolling/ For ground &Back Ground (the sound will be the same but toned differently for the impression of depth) /On-off/SoundAnAcReES-001.

-AnAcReEs-002 / bullet impact / F&B / On-Off / SoundAnAcReEs-002.

-AnAcReEs-003/Sniper rifle Sound walking (the clicking sound of a rifle when the character is running or walking)/For Ground/On-Off/SoundAnAcReEs-003.

The fourth list make it the voices. Call it Animation Voices Essential Characters. For example .

-AnVoEsCroud-001(the sound of the different voices in the crowd that bring it alive)/Back Ground/Always on/SoundAnVoEsCround-001.

-AnVoEsBobyB1-001(The voice of the main character during the B1 animation.)/For Ground/On-Off/SoundAnVoBobyA1-001.

The fifth list is all about the menu and other details. Call it Animation Essentials XXXX . This list will have categories of objects in it. For example:

-AnEsP90(MachineGunP90)-001/F&B/On-Off/SoundAnEsP90-001.(the firing Sound)

-AnEsP90(Silencer)-002/For Ground/On-Off/SoundAnEsP90-002.

-An EsP90(Clicking noise)-003/F&B/On-Off/SoundAnEsP90-003

This process is fastidious but not too complicated. Make sure to put in the lists all the necessary material for all the synchronization of the game. Organize them according to your own logic but keep a key method.

At this point, it is time for the team to go out there a make three new friends, a sound director/engineer ,a talented 3D animator and programmer savy in video game engines.

Animation

Now the team should have six members, The 3D designer busy creating the models. Assisted by the drawer to keep a direction of the art translating in to graphics. The animator should have all the material he needs, plus all the animation list to start putting the models in motion. Also assisted by the art directors to give a good lively translation into animation. And the sound director a full list of all that he needs to engineer for the game. The programmer on his side should start looking at the best way to put all this in the appropriate game engine and start creating the first DLL files.

For now keep in mind that the main objective is to be able to put together a representation of the first level of the game in the computer. What we called a "tetra" demo earlier. So the producer must make a list of all the work that needs to be done in each field to accomplish this first step. Do not worry about elaborate 3D animations for the "A" story. Ask the drawer to make some nice animations scenes to cover this parts. Just focus on all the needs for the tetra demo.

The following is an essentials guide line for the animations. That the team must focus on at this level of the production.

For Sports game , animation is first all about the coherence of the camera animation. To zoom and fallowing the ball. Or give nice slow motions and what not. The second point is to make sure that the body language of the players delivers the proper effect. If the game is an adaptation of humor , then those guys must really move funny. If the game is pro, then the athlete must look really dashing and project the feeling of super-heroes at work. In addition the animation of the crowd and the benches is the essential back ground animation so it must be used and look very appealing. Also the animations of the menus and the scores must have some special effects, like on TV.

-For puzzle and card games, the animation is all about the fluidity of the pieces moving around. It must be perfect. In addition animations of flares and "bling" must be added very professionally to those pieces so they look alive on the screen. For this type of game the animation is all about precision work. The back ground of the game and its eventual animations. Must be directed towards displaying the most exquisite kind of graphic art. That might require some light animations.

-For car games, the animation is all about reflections , flares and light special effects. Most game engines for cars are all geared up for this work. But the precision work on the color-palette animations is what will give the quality of the speed sensation. The menus also require some serious animations for this type of game. Animations on how the engines work from the inside out. To show the air in the turbo cycling and other things as such. And if characters are present in the game, make sure they don't walk around like sticks.

-For strategy games, animations is all about adding social interactions and city life. There is no end here , the more the better.

There is extra work to make sure that the individuals have different types of body languages. Animation here will be also about making sure that the screen is clear with all that activity . That the eye can understand what he sees, it sound obvious, but it might get tricky. Also add a lot of nice special effect with the sun light and sky activity.

To animate more the grounds, make animations of wild life. Dears popping out and sprinting, wolf packs hunting, eagles preying. Use all you can input. (May be they could have a Bigfoot sighting occasionally).The inventory and the menus will require some animation work to polish the genre. The menus are part of the game-play so they must be perfected to the outmost.

-For all types of RPGs, the list of animations is quite large. But they are not too complex. The first thing to set right is the animation of the camera moving as the character walks around. It must shake so to reflect the appropriate posture or walking mode. Then focus on the animation of the hands that are visible from a first person point of view. They must look very much alive and have some nice independent finger animations. Once you have the animations for the characters momentum modes. Spend time going through the levels and add back ground animations just like in a strategy game. You must then deal with the animation of all the characters that are independently acting on their own in the game

RPGs are filled with people so they must all have a different type of behavior and body language. It is always better to have different types of body bearings it intensifies the production value. Then it is time to pay attention to all types of light special effects that will dress the game. This animation work must be artistic. Keep it in mind, it is all about displaying graphic quality and eye pleasing sceneries.

Also spend time polishing the small animations that are required for the weapons in the hands of the character. Clearly show all sorts of cocking devices and light effects for the guns, and also the recoil effects for each specific weapon. In this process complete also the animation for magic and spells often drawn by the left hand.

The next step is to get on with the details of the enemies animations during combat. The point is to have the enemies behave like a real team. Different actions for the artificial intelligence are to be created here. Hiding for cover, signaling each other for changing covers. Jumping and rolling to dodge. Give the alarm , and the occasional guy who is goanna freak out a make a mess. The behavior of the enemies is part of the game-play so it is important to pay attention to dress this angle as much as possible.

Now it is time to do all the animations for guns. The canon fire, the cocking devices, and the ammo flowing out. And the light effects on the weapons. Also spend time for the impact animations. Make them fluid and realistic with the fire rate. And spend time on all the reaction effects of destruction on the scenery for bullet storms. Explosion and fires must look also appropriate for the cinematic effects of the game during game-play.

The Animation of the enemies falling and dying in various way must have some nice acting to add to the drama of the game. This is a very important point to polish.

For all type of games, after all those details are partitioned and created. The last step is light animations to make the color pallets look even more awesome. The animation is the same approach for big and small devices. Except that for small devices the games are going to be limited in memory. There for it is even more important to blow peoples mind away.

Polishing the Content of the game

If the producer really loves video-games, he will probably come up with a very good story for the game. But that does not mean that he would have the skill to write properly the dialogues of the game. In case of a game with an elaborate story, it is a part of the main objective to give the characters their own particularities that make them special. So the aspect of their speech, must always be dressed like a good writer would. All the side stories of an RPG must also present their own aspect of intrigue and plot. Spending time to make the side stories as cool as possible will require some extra work as the game comes together.

But as an Example if the project is a puzzle of any sorts, the key to the story polish, would be to use the cadence of the puzzle to make the story character move on a story-line. To make the character jump or take any other action. The player must make a particular achievement in the puzzle. So the game would present two modes minimum. A first "Pro" mode very challenging, with some nice "bling". And a second "arcade" mode where the game is more played like a game of blitz in chess. So the puzzle has two game-plays into one game,(an extra game-play with the purpose of the avatar).

For simulations, the lack of a story mode is always a negative. A story mode could be used for the player to experience the universe of that Game. Imagine a good car simulation, with a story mode where you represent the driver. In this case , the driver is a secret agent who must get his mission done and win the champion ship because he can. So each level would end with a race that he must win. The story could be place in the racing universe of the 60's. But the simulation "mode" be of modern composition. This kind of story telling for simulation is often missing. It would fit for hand device simulations , to mix game play. As often games for small devices are limited in story and scale.

For strategy games the presence of a good story is always a plus. Just like an RPG it would require proper writing, but in strategy the stories can take biblical proportions, that's what is appealing for this genre. And if the game is designed to be a killer for essentially on-line multiplayer. Then the occasional production of some stories for the game to be played in solo mode, is a perfect way to keep the game's notoriety alive over time, with awesome story telling.

The writing of a plot for hand devices is a bit different. The story must be experienced with a more dynamic pace and a more straight to the point writing. Due to screen size and memory limitations. And also because games for hand devices must have an arcade aspect to it as they appeal for quick game-plays. But the best way to use a back ground story for any kind of hand device; is to use it to make the junction between the different platforms. Bring together the hand devices platform and the on-line community gaming using personal computers.

Let take for example a game based on fighting. The classic arcade type of game with multiple contenders. In this case once the player has acquired the app for the game. He would get access to a site on internet to build his own personalized character, (or characters as it is often the case.) Then he could export the character from the site to his hand device, and have it to play in the game as a custom contender.

In addition to the fighting levels of the original game. Then the player could download to his hand devices apps to train the character. Like a gym, or nice levels. The player could experience his character going on an platform adventure. Where he will get some nice drama and aptitude upgrades. And the use of a gym to repeatedly train your character is in fact a classic in the genre. These examples would all be additional apps to the game.

All of the most popular on-line games have very complicated and very long design of progression for the characters. In some games it could take years to work your way up to have an awesome character. So the idea is for the player to be able to take his avatars with him "out of the house", and be able to train them on his phone and have a variety of solo adventures. Experience all type of arcade game-play on the phone. Then import the avatar back to the on-line community.

And have a blast in competitions or some team adventures with some thrilling 3D graphics. The point is to bring in one big video-game hand device gaming; and perfect 3D gaming on personal computers or consoles. (For this type of venture the producer will need a full team of writers to come up with nice plots all the time.)

The Secret Kung-Fu

The producer's secret kung-fu is the perception of all the synchronizations to be accomplished for the game. That's what his focus is all about. Synchronicity, is the ability to make all the creation process fit into one another like Russian dolls. And implement the creative process in such a way, that the game will have a whole unique ambiance and art directing. All the details of the story; the animations , the game-play, fit each other like an enzyme with it's protein. Which is like "Mega" production value for the impact of a game on the market.

-First; keep good "sync" for organizing the files and the notes, in the order of their creation. To always have the whole vision in mind. Keep a journal with the list of all you need to get achieved, from each member of the team. Written step by step from the beginning to the end of the project. (Last objective of the list: "Party at Maui with the crew".)

-"Sync" for the creation of the time-lines; and the correlations between them. Their precision and size, will change constantly for adaptations needed. So they must make must make sense and be easy to alter. This is the main part of producing. (The producer's main work)

-Story-lines synchronization. Direct the plot adaptation so that all the different stories come together quite efficiently with interesting side plots, and good dialogues . The use of a ghost writer for this effect is highly recommended.

-the production chain must be optimized so that the team's work will complete each other . Make a listing of the planning process, to map the production line in that effect. Keep always track of where you stand in the creation process from the first step to the full demo. All the first efforts should be directed to have a tetra demo as soon as possible.

-Make sure that the first creations of the maps, are not too messy. And that the first drafts have the right contents already in them.

The creation of those map must also fallow a type of design. So that the insertions of the time-lines events on the maps and levels; gives a precise idea of what's is going on in those areas. The work on the maps and level drafts is going to be continuous in sync with the time-lines. So it must get looking more a more pro after each draft.

-Work closely with your art director, so that the creation of the characters and all the needs to fill the game are in tune with the "artistic" vision of the adaptation. The first draft on paper of the characters and all the other drawings, will be part of the packaging for the game. So they must also look net quickly. Sometimes the responsibility of the art directing adaptations will fall on the producer. For some particular need in the levels, the artists might not be able to get the whole vision. Because their imagination might get limited about video-games. So take time to communicate with them and make the paper drawings look as good as possible.

-Always look for ideas to use the game's graphics to help the story telling. Just like in the production of a movie; here it is all about perfect set and art directing. Everything in the graphics must relate to the story. And have the appropriate intonation of lighting and content according to the drama. This type of art directing in Hollywood on studio sets is super expensive. But graphics are cheap, so get as creative as possible. There are 3D libraries available on the internet, where you can buy 3D models of any kind. It is highly recommended to use those libraries. If there are royalty issue to use the material for profit , it is not a problem just adapt the models to your needs.

-Make sure that the transition from the original pictures and drawings into graphics, will carry the actual original artistic value of the project. This could be a difficult step because of the system limitations , if you are designing for a small device. But if you must make sacrifices; make sure not to dent the synchronicity of the game itself.

-Always keep your mind open for new ideas about all sorts of animations that would fit the game. Never hesitated to just insert a new idea for an animation at any point of the making. Think of animations about the enemies and everything that could give a sense of personality to all the different characters. The more difference you can give the player in basic animations, the better the game.

And add some dialogues between the enemies. Like good jokes or something really gross . Have fun re-imagining the characters and bringing them to life.

-Do the same work for the back ground. Always look for new inputs of climate, wild life or else. Like cats preying on rats in the ruins, or all sorts of details that will come to you, as you dive deeper into the creative process.

Make sure to keep a side list of all this synchronization details that will pop in your mind. Those small details are "Gold" for production value.

-During the whole process , the producer must make sure that each time that something is being re-drawn, or re-worked in any way; it will come closer to perfection.

 All the notes, all the meshes and all the hand creations, will be part of the presentation packaging. They must reflect in their creation a very professional aspect.

-The producer is going to have to keep the team tight together. So it is important to first organize the time and the space for the work to be done.

But also make sure to organize time for social interaction between the team. It is important that everybody becomes good "buds" and starts to see the project as a serious future for themselves. Pick your team carefully make sure everybody will get along. And don't hesitate to broaden your horizons by meeting new people for the project. If you could get additional 3D animators and designers that would only be for the better.

-The producer is going to keep asking for add-ons that sound very simple; but they are a lot of work on the team. And the team members have a single focus; each on their task. Very quickly the producer can become the enemy because he keeps asking for things but he doesn't do much. There for it is important to communicate your "kung-fu" very gently to the team. And take some time to understand the human factors about team management.

Chapter 3

Optimizing production for market reach and maximum appeal

To do list:

-Get the tetra demo up and running. Make it as elaborate as possible.

-Expose the tetra demo on the blogs. And make a "real" (like actor) for the game with all the contents. Art material and team included.

-Collect funds from investors if you already can.

-Keep pushing production to complete a full demo of the first level. Fully playable.

-Optimize production with the marketing tips. Make the project as appealing as you can.

-Start looking for a professional company that can help to adapt the game for different hand devices. And eventually distribution of the finished app.

-Package your game and seek for a bank loan.

Crew & team work

To build up your team, you will have to use the social medias in a smart way. Today there are blogs about everything. So first find your drawer/art-director by reaching out on the net.(If you don't have one.). And use his work to communicate your project on the blogs with some real material. Keep scouting all the blogs and specialized site about the material and talents you need. If your communications skills are good and the project is cool. Provided with some nice first drawing, you will find a lot of guys out there just like you, who would love to get on your ride. All you must do is show intent and purpose as a serious team leader and producer.   Plus there are now a lot of internet site, that are just in the business of exposing projects like this and find investments. They do very well, so you must get your project in those sites as soon as possible.

The good news is that all the softwares and plug-ins that the team will need to make the project, are available via internet for a monthly fee. As the point is to budget funds for only what is directly related to creation. This makes the access to the best software very simple and quite affordable. While looking for your team , you could have for requirement that they will all have the software that they need. Or the producer could start budgeting the amount that he will need for the project. Both ways it is important that the team feels that they are going to be considered as partners and not employees. The idea is to gather a team that can work on the project for free on spare time over the agreement that they will get a share of the profits. (Unless the producer is already fully funded to hire a team on a payroll full time.) So the producer must be on the top of his game as a leader, organizing the time and space for the crew to work and advance forward on the project becoming a "band of brothers".

Keep in mind that the objective here is not just to make a game; but to get in the industry. And then make even better games with more resources available. So if it all works out; you will need a team close to you with all the experience needed to take over the head of all the different departments of your future company. Because once you are in; you will need a team of a hundred or more to create games of pure awesomeness.

As you move forward in the creation of the games, the producer must also start a blog about the game's concept. And so collect more creative inputs of any kind. And even find extra help for details that can get annoying. Making a social network about the project as you go along is the producer's job, it's the mission. It will help you meet all the geniuses you need. And can even become a source for funding before you know it.

For efficiency in a project like this, the production line's synchronization is everything. If the artist just finished the drawing of the main character then the sound engineer should be already working on his voice, and the animator making an animation for him using a dummy. As soon as the 3D designer finishes the meshes for the main character; from the original drawings, you will already have something functional for the demo. And material for the blog to show the production's coherence to attract investors. Understanding this methodology and applying it, is crucial.

Production : Simplify

If you are going for an elaborate game of any genre .The best way to get it done is to see your game in two steps. First step is to adapt it for a perfect game on hand devices in order to get the game out there the fastest and the most efficiently. Then , once you have the money to create your company, you can go for the second step and expand the concept in 3D for consoles and multiplayer.

Game apps sold on phone and tablets are very popular. And the distribution for apps is very simple, and puts you immediately in the "cloud" for marketing. To be present in the cloud with a finished product for sale, is in itself quite a accomplishment. Because of the size of the market and the reach through the cloud, you will find yourself exposed in the market almost exponential. So all things being equal; if the game cuts it right, you will make sells immediately.

To adapt a big RPG adventure-action game on a hand device. The best way is to make a mix of 3D and 2D. The backgrounds are 2D top-notch pictures, with a sharp high geometric perspective. The characters are smaller on the screen, and are all made in nice 3D. The characters can move on the map (that is a picture), in regard of the perspective. If the picture has the perspective of a deep, large hall from a frontal view.

Then the characters get smaller as they run toward the exit at the end of the screen . And they get larger as they run forward in to the tunnel towards the screen.

Each time the characters exit the scene, you switch to another picture with a different perspective, and so forth. What comes out very nicely is to have all the object in the scene that the avatar can interact with also in 3D. Contrasting the color palette of the background , with the color palette of the 3D animation it can give a very nice touch of cool ambiance to the game.

This methodology of "geometric-perspective" to simulate space; can also be used to insert some levels that are action platform game-play, and others that are pure shooting and some for exploring. This example of production aspect is a perfect way to make a game using different types of game-play for a hand device. And to tell a good story at the same time.

 The same approach can be used for a action platform-arcade or even car games. Keep in mind that the production value is all about the art directing and the high quality of the background universe.

There are a lot of very talented artist who are perusing the creation of a comic books. To be totally honest, they don't do very well. The comic book industry is a tight "market niche" and very difficult. But it has all the contents to design good games of any sorts. To adapt a comic book to this type of video-game production is good logic. The game play will come with the story, as the character is going to have super powers. And the story line should come out quite awesome, as comic book writers have good imagination.

The pace of the plot in comic books, is fast and intriguing. Exactly like the need for hand devices in which the story pace must be quick and appealing. So to simplify production, it is recommended to find a comic book designer with a project of his own. And bring your two works together, so he would be the art director of the game.

Plus a finished brand new comic book would be the perfect way to expose the game on the blogs. And also a "Ace" for the presentation package.

Optimizing Production

As you begin designing your game it is important to incorporate in the creative process some smart incentives to be make the game more efficient for its market impact and financial success. For the next conceptualization recommendations; you could use fighting , driving, sports, fantasy sports-teams; pretty much any type of game-play. So as you build the game, keep in mind some of the tips that fallow.

The game must have a multiplayer aspect of at least two player one on one using their hand device. So that the players can win or lose their eventual avatars. This kind of approach is very similar to the card games for kids. If it is extended to a simple kind of game on a hand device not as complicated as they get on line, this aspect of gaming can even bring financial benefits to the player. If the game is quick and the art directing is awesome, then probably people would start exchanging characters and even sell them. Or buy gears for their avatars for a couple of quarters. Obviously the art directing and all the aspects of the game must cut it right, but the challenge is to make a fun game-play so people can enjoy quickly playing the game. The point is to give the player an immediate sense of control and empowerment playing. Like if wining feels "God-Like".

The quality and the extent to which the player can personalize his avatar are the second key to the success here. In that effect, as the operating systems are limited on hand devices, then after buying the app; players go on line to the game community to make their avatar for free. In this on-line universe, everything is possible to engineer. The difference is that the on-line community is essentially used to create and exchange or make tournaments, meet people and so. The idea is to keep the on-line gaming simple and accessible for people who don't spend hours and hours building up their characters. If the on-line community and games evolves and become as complicated as all the others, without losing the player base. Then the game became something else, and you can consider yourself an "Ace".

One other major aspect to optimize your production on hand devices is the promotion for company coupons , discounts, or free minutes on cell-phones. Basically, make a free app-game that is fun and where the player can collect as bonuses or achievements, loads of actual coupons and other cool stuff. It could be just 10c for discount or 25sec free for the phone. The idea is that it would be cumulative.

So one player would get the app and then for instance, use his member ship card number from a store, to play a game loaded with goodies from that store. And then the score points would go to his card account for discount. The idea is a bit challenging because of the reach to the main retail companies and getting them to play ball. But it would also be a perfect platform for advertising their discounts and promotions. As the games target all different types of consumers at the same time. From family guys just playing for fun to young chicks hunting for shoe promotions. A new standard for retail businesses to make promotions and others discounts can be achieved.

Imagine playing on-line with a personalized race car on your cell phone provider's "gaming promotion-platform". And this year you have collected points and minutes that you have not cashed in yet, saving up for a new phone. That is the cool kind of appeal for the consumer to play the game regularly. On the track and the game's universe, the retailers can put all the advertising and other contents as they wish; so they get to expose their material with variety and precision.

As another example, imagine a treasure hunt for an annual 15000 dollar gift card with maximum of 100 players. Each players must pay a fee of 10 bucks to enter the treasure hunt. The same concept can be used with flag games and last man standing challenges.

Even virtual casinos where people can gamble their cell-phone points and free minutes with other individuals. It sounds crazy, but people are goanna go nuts on it, especially on hand devices with a quick game-play. (Picture Mum gambling the coupons and free minutes collected by the kids; while keeping an eye on them doing their home work. That's a solid family!)

Big retail companies would not put the money down to do this all on their own. And big video game companies would have to over stretch their actual business model to do so, so they do not pursue this idea. But the retail companies would immediately start working with someone who can provide this service with quality and precision. Plus, having people to log on their site to update their coupons account and what not; is an absolute need in their business plan model.

The accomplishment of this concept would make the producer a very rich man indeed. As it brings with the concept a perpetual advertisement platform.

Getting Funds to complete the project

Earlier in the book we mentioned the concept of a tetra demo. The tetra demo is a composition with the games first pieces to give an impression of the game. It does not require the programming of the game-play or other elaborate inputs. The importance of the tetra demo is that it can already be used to look for funds as the project unfolds.

It is the perfect material to expose on those numerous sites that help people find investors for cool projects. The idea is to show a real project that is already completely under design and very serious in its intent for accomplishment. Keep the demo and the material updated as you go; and talk to the people on the sites who will ask for information and show interest in your project. This very brand new method for financing is doing miracles and it is perfect for individual entrepreneurs. You might be surprised by the positive response you will get.

Another use for the tetra demo is to take an appointment with a company that makes apps for phones. There are a variety of those company out there, so approach one with the project and ask for the amount of funds necessary to contract them to finishing the project with all the material that you have produced. This is a smart move; you can keep control on the quality of the game as you are the contractor, and use a professional company that can ensure the quality of the programming for different phone interfaces. In fact; sooner or later the use of such company is going to be needed for the adaptation of the game to all the different types of phones and tablets out there.

At this point you can ask for the amount to the investors on the internet. Or you can also take your project, go to the bank and apply for a loan. If you package a tetra demo, and show all the material and planning process of the game already executed. And in addition, you show to the banker that the money you want is to fund the creation of the game, with a company that you have already found and that will help with distribution, you will get your loan.

Keep in mind that even if you can make the whole game as a finished product with your team, the need for funds will be necessary for marketing and adapting the game to different interfaces. Yet if the game is good and playable , (and stable on at least one system;) it would be very easy to distribute the game. Big phone companies provide the service of distribution for apps of any kind on their platforms. All you need is to contact them and show them your app.

In conclusion, this book is to help understand that if a person enjoys video-games. Then the idea of the game to be made is almost immediate in his mind. And probably pretty good as it comes from a gamers mind. The Challenge is the planning process to keep a clear list of the little details that must be covered. This hand book is to help lining the planning process to get started from the beginning to the end. And start producing. The best option is to reach out to other people like you who are passionate and willing to do the same thing. The good news is to make a game for hand devices requires a small team. Argo, reaching out on the internet to find your team and financing is only logical. I encourage all devoted gamers to get on this quest and start living their dreams.

Made in United States
Troutdale, OR
11/17/2023